Acknowledgement

I would like to thank all the people who have supported me in all aspects of my life – personally, professionally, and creatively. Special thanks to my father, who has always been my biggest inspiration and teacher. Also, I'd like to thank my son who keeps me motivated to be a better person and make this world a better place.

Dedication

I dedicate this book to my son Roland, my shining star.

About The Author

Elliot "Solar" Fisher is very passionate about the ocean and keeping our planet clean. Since 2009, he has worked as a Solar Energy Professional and been an advocate for renewable energy. He comes from a family of educators and is motivated to spread the message of conservation and sustainability. As a California native, Elliot enjoys surfing along the Pacific Coast and traveling to new destinations. He loves music and is an avid musician. He is a dedicated father and wants to help protect our environment for our future generations.

www.SolarFisher.com

Rise and shine! It's a brand new day, with so many things to do and places to explore. Let's see what's happening on the ocean floor.

"Good morning, octopus. Would you like to play?"
"No, Stevie, I am busy. Now excuse me; I will be on my way."

Look at the dolphins surfing the waves; it looks more fun than sitting in caves. I wish I could join, but I might get stuck in the trash. The dolphins are not worried as they leap high and splash.

Playing in the water is the thing that I love the most.
Is it just me, or does this water seem gross?
"I will find cleaner water and swim across the ocean.
Goodbye Stevie, I am already in motion."

The garbage in the ocean is getting out of hand.
I will head to the beach and relax in the sand.

Oh no! There is so much trash here too. I will ask my ant friends; they will know just what to do. "We are busy, Stevie. Stop causing a commotion, don't bother us, and go back to the ocean!"

I am very small, but the giraffe is tall, like a tree. Maybe I will ask if he can help me. "Sorry, Stevie, not today. Maybe you can ask the lion; he is right over that way."

"I came from the sea where the water was filled with pollution. Maybe we can work together and find a solution?"
The lion looked around and noticed all of the trash, but he was hungry and needed to eat, so he quickly made a dash.

Everyone seems so busy; I better try another place. The world needs help, and there is no time to waste. I will take a trip across the sky; I better hold on tight, I don't know how to fly.

Excuse me, Bee, but did you hear the news?
"Go away, Stevie. Can't you see I am taking a snooze?"

Stevie climbed up high and shouted, "There is something you must know!" The bird didn't listen, "Sorry Stevie, but I gotta go."

I came from the sea and traveled across the land. Wherever I go, no one seems to understand. I went to the beach, the jungle, and even the sky, but no one wanted to listen; it makes me want to cry. I wish I could make a difference...

Stevie looked up and saw one star that shined so bright; it was the brightest star that lit up the night. He thought, "That is a special star, and I am a star too. Tomorrow morning, I know just what I will do."

The very next morning, Stevie decided to make the world a better place. He didn't rely on anyone; he just went at his own pace.

There was much work to be done, but Stevie did it with a smile.
He cleaned the garbage on the beach, mile after mile.

Stevie was determined to make the world clean and neat; he wouldn't stop until the job was complete.

Stevie worked very hard no matter the day or weather, the other animals noticed, and they soon came together.

The changes Stevie made were very drastic,
so the sea animals wanted to join and help
clean up the trash and plastic.

The positive change spread from the sea to the land.
Now, all of the animals wanted to help lend a hand.

Everyone joined together as one big team.
The world was improving, and it felt like a wonderful dream.

The animals all worked together,
big and small. No matter how wide, no matter how tall.

The sky was blue, and the water was clean,
plants and trees all around, growing healthy and green.

Stevie may have been a small starfish, but he didn't let anything stop him, and he got his wish.

Stevie's wish came true, which gave him great satisfaction, he never knew it would cause such a huge reaction. The changes he made spread far beyond the sand, up high in the sky, and all across the land. The positive energy went very, very far. Stevie, you definitely are one shining star!

©Copyright 2023 Elliot Fisher All Rights Reserved

Made in the USA
Las Vegas, NV
23 December 2023